TAKE ME TO THE WATER

IMMERSION BAPTISM IN VINTAGE MUSIC AND PHOTOGRAPHY 1890–1950

PHOTOGRAPHS FROM THE COLLECTION OF JIM LINDERMAN

ESSAYS BY JIM LINDERMAN AND LUC SANTE

NOTES ON SONGS AND SERMONS BY STEVEN LANCE LEDBETTER

SONGS AND SERMONS FROM 1924–1940

from the collections of Joe Bussard, Steven Lance Ledbetter,

Frank Mare and Roger Misiewicz

DUST-TO-DIGITAL

ATLANTA, GEORGIA

2009

DENOMINATION BLUES

WASHINGTON PHILLIPS

Well, denominations has no right to fight
They oughta just treat each other right
And that's all, I tell you that's all
But you better have Jesus, I tell you that's all

The Primitive Baptists, they believe
You can't get to Heaven unless you wash your feet
And that's all, I tell you that's all
But you better have Jesus, I tell you that's all

The only Primitive that has any part
Is the one that's at the washing with the feeling heart
And that's all, I tell you that's all
But you better have Jesus, I tell you that's all

Now the Missionary Baptists they believe
Go under the water and not to wash his feet
And that's all, I tell you that's all
But you better have Jesus, I tell you that's all

Now the Indian Methodists they believe
Sprinkle the head and not to wash the feet
And that's all, I tell you that's all
But you better have Jesus, I tell you that's all

Now the African Methodists they believe the same
'Cause they know their denomination ain't a thing but a name
And that's all, I tell you that's all
But you better have Jesus, I tell you that's all

INTRODUCTION

JIM LINDERMAN

Record collectors and photograph collectors share many traits. Both flip through racks and boxes, both seek to preserve things of our past which have been relegated and both have personal, private drives which get them out of bed early on the right days. If you have ever been in line at a flea market and observed the darting eyes of those at the front, you would swear collecting has a genetic component. However, the nature of collecting has changed much since I began putting together this group of photos. What once took months is now possible with a stored search on an auction website. Seemingly rare objects have been found to be common. Authenticity has become elusive, personal mementos have been replaced with merchandise created to act as such and many important, beautiful objects are forever lost. Without the vision and passion of collectors, a great deal of our visual and auditory heritage would not exist. Thankfully, private collectors are often willing to share their finds, and today is certainly the richest environment to experience the past product of our artists and performers, even if it is being seen and heard in digital rather than physical form. We are

lucky to have publishers and reissue labels packaging this precious material in forms which stand out among the cyber-clutter, which bring it to new eyes and ears and even create valuable collectibles for the future.

I believe there is an undefined but present relationship between the visual and aural in many art forms. Artists often work harder when depicting spiritual themes and musicians in the service of the Lord often turn in the best performances. Were the photographers "on the clock" when they took these pictures, or did they too feel the beauty and passion being drawn before their eyes? Did the performers recorded here reach for a higher stan-

dard when they played their gospel songs? I would like to think so. It would help explain the spiritually charged, emotional and powerful results.

Thanks go to my wife Janna Rosenkranz, who has the wisdom to let me be exactly who I am. Jimmy Allen, whose harrowing book *Without Sanctuary* was the inspiration for this collection of photos. The late painter Sterling Strauser, who once told me to "collect the heck" out of what I found interesting, trust my judgment over the suggestions of dealers and that if I lost sleep over an object I should go back in the morning and buy it. Robert Reeves, who understands that "cool things" are found in unlikely places. Tanya Heinrich at the American Folk Art Museum, Brian Wallis at the International Center of Photography. Erin Flanagan, Delia Congram, Joan Gilbertson, and Sheryl Colyer each in their own way the smartest people I know. Most of all my parents. Oh …and the many teachers in my life who finally just gave up and sent me to the library.

TAKE ME TO THE WATER

LUC SANTE

The first time I saw an image of a river baptism it was in a photograph taken in Texas, sometime around 1900. No, actually, what I meant to say was that the first time I saw such an image it was probably an illustration showing John the Baptist pouring water over the head of Jesus, standing in the River Jordan, and that illustration was undoubtedly in the missal I employed as a child. I was raised Catholic, was baptized at five days old by a priest who poured a thin stream of water over my head as he held me over a font in the baptistry of a church, and for many years was only glancingly aware of the practice of river baptism as it continues to this day.

When I saw the photograph from Texas, though, I was overwhelmed by the serene beauty of the scene, and its strangeness. I had been thinking about images of worship in photography, curious about the fact that historically there have been so few—cameras were seldom welcome at services in the past, and the standard photograph of a religious community tended to show the pastor and congregants standing, often stiffly, in front of the church. The image of river baptism, by contrast, seemed to radi-ate the very qualities enjoyed by participants in the scene. In addition, it immediately registered as an iconographic category—the rare sort of image that is infinitely replicable and unambiguously identifiable, while at the same time guaranteeing that no two examples will be quite the same. I knew at once that I would never tire of seeing pictures of river baptisms, and began seeking them out. When I finally saw Jim Linderman's extraordinary collection, I recognized that my instincts were correct.

Sometimes there are only two people in the water, the preacher and the candidate, and sometimes there are many: a large collective baptism. Sometimes the candidates wear their ordinary clothes; sometimes they are obviously in their Sunday best; sometimes—generally when the subjects are African American—the candidates wear long white robes, often with white head coverings. Most times the scene is a river, but sometimes it might be some other body of water, including the ocean, and now and then the setting is a man-made pool. Baptisms most often take place in the warm months, but you do see images in which all the spectators on the banks are wearing overcoats, and

from the *Chicago Defender* (National edition); November 20, 1926

there is one here in which the ceremony is occurring in a hole chopped in the ice cover of a stream. The scene is usually tranquil, blissful, although a few are unruly, when all involved have been seized by uncontrollable holy passion. Sometimes the camera looks over the shoulders of the crowd, in the position of a congregant; other times everyone faces the camera, which has become a participant. Most of the pictures here date from the first half of the twentieth century. Not a few of them are scarred, bent, water-damaged, even torn, which is reflective only of the fact that its original owners led hard lives, ones that included inadequate housing, multiple moves, ad hoc storage, and perhaps fires, floods—calamities to which the prints have borne mute witness.

The practice of baptism has been subject to considerable controversy, at least since the Protestant Reformation. It is a feature of nearly every Christian sect, but nearly every aspect of it is subject to differing interpretations. Many denominations practice infant baptism; many deem baptism a sacrament, a condition for full membership as well as a prerequisite for salvation; many consider sprinkling a few drops or pouring a thin stream over the head to be sufficient. The sects that practice full-immersion or submersion baptism also restrict baptism to adults, or at least congregants above the age of reason. They are the Apostolic Brethren; the Baptists; the Christadelphians; the Churches of Christ; the Jehovah's Witnesses; the various "Holiness" churches,

such as the Assemblies of God; the Pentecostals; the Revivalists; and the Seventh-Day Adventists. (The Church of Jesus Christ of Latter-Day Saints also practices full-immersion baptism of adults, but its theology differs so much from every other group that it effectively belongs in a separate category.) For all but the Baptists and the Seventh-Day Adventists the ritual spiritually regenerates the recipient. The Apostolic Brethren, the Christadelphians, and the Jehovah's Witnesses baptize only in Jesus's name; all others do so in the name of the Trinity. For those three denominations as well as the Churches of Christ and the Revivalists, baptism is necessary for salvation, and the Seventh-Day Adventists further specify that while baptism is a prerequisite for salvation, it is not the way thereto. The Baptists, the Holiness churches, and the Pentecostals engage in what is called believer's baptism, which is a ritual of faith, an affirmation of belief, not a requirement for salvation but a mark of adhesion.

Generally, churches carry out baptisms in places that have been so employed for many years, that have accrued layers of association and sentiment and in which the current is gentle, the bottom is reasonably firm, and the water is not above waist-deep. Before the ceremony, deacons wade out and determine a propitious spot, then drive in three stakes that will serve to delimit the arc in which the ritual will occur. The candidates, who may or may not be wearing white robes bound at the waist and knees

"Old Time Baptism"

BY REV. R. M. MASSEY

The well-known Reverend Massey has put lots of inspiration into this Paramount Record No. 12618, "Old Time Baptism," parts 1 and 2. You will rejoice as you hear those who are being baptized profess their faith in the Lord, and you can't help but feel uplifted and better for having this beautiful and inspiring record in your home. Ask your dealer for No. 12618, or send us the coupon.

12618—Old Time Baptism, Part 1, and **Old Time Baptism**, Part 2; Sermons by Rev. R. M. Massey.

from *the Chicago Defender* (National edition); May 12, 1928

(for practical reasons but also symbolic of the bounds of sin, which will be loosened after the ceremony has transpired), are led out into the water by deacons. The minister wades out separately while the congregation sings, then delivers a brief sermon. One by one the candidates are brought to the minister, who joins the candidate's hands in prayer, covers his or her face, utters a statement of baptism in the name of Jesus or the Trinity, then submerges the candidate for a moment. Each person baptized leaves the water separately, is enfolded in towels, and retreats behind a screen to change clothes before returning to witness the remaining baptisms.

The ceremony, which usually concludes with a sermon and may be followed by an assembly at the church, is accompanied throughout by hymns, as well as more spontaneous effusions: tears, shouts, exhortations. The novelist and folklorist Dorothy Scarborough described an African-American ceremony she witnessed in the South in the 1920s:

> With each immersion the excitement grew, the shouting became more wild and unrestrained, the struggles of the candidate more violent. Women ran up and down the banks of the pond, wringing their hands, groaning and crying…. The crowd surged back and forth, and as one bystander would rush to greet a candidate coming out of the water, shrieking forth joy and thanksgiving, the crowd would join in vehement song. Sometimes half a dozen shouters would be in ecstasy at once, each surrounded by a group of admirers trying to control him, or her—usually her. Each group would be a center of commotion in the general excitement. The shouter would fall on the ground, writhing about as if in anguish, tearing her hair, beating off those who sought to calm her.

—*On the Trail of Negro Folk-Songs*, Cambridge, MA: Harvard University Press, 1925, pp. 15-16

Whether you have ever actually experienced a baptism or not, whether you are a believer or not, these pictures and the music that accompanies them transmit all the emotional information: the excitement and the serenity, the fellowship and the warmth, the wind and the water. They are about theater, pageantry, holiday, inclusion, transformation, enveloping love and transporting joy. They show a great many people in the midst of one of the peak experiences of their lives. Even the calmest scenes are electrified by the ecstasy of their actors. You would have to have a heart of tin not to recognize this as one of the happiest collections of archival photographs ever assembled.

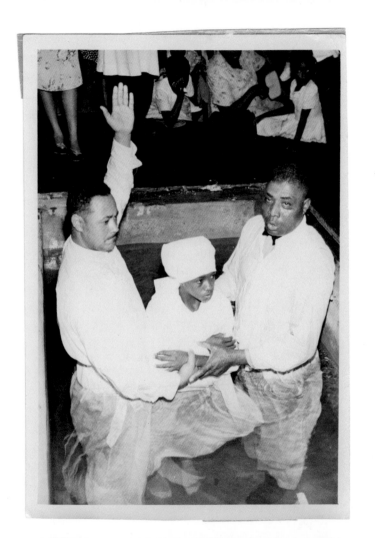

NEGRO BAPTISMAL CEREMONY IN THE POTOMAC

        EIGHTY NEGROES WERE BAPTIZED IN THE POTOMAC RIVER, WASHINGTON, D. C., JUNE 21, IN A SPECTACULAR CEREMONY HELD BY THE CHURCH OF GOD. PHOTO SHOWS CONVERTS IN THE WATER WHILE SONG SERVICES ARE BEING BROADCAST FROM THE BAPTISMAL BARGE OVER THE RADIO.

Photo.
Art Gallery

C. E. Peterson,
Carson, Nev.

Pictures enlarged and finished in any stlye.

1895

Baptism — who? where?

Baptismal scene
at Battle Creek

OWL
PHOTO
DEPT.

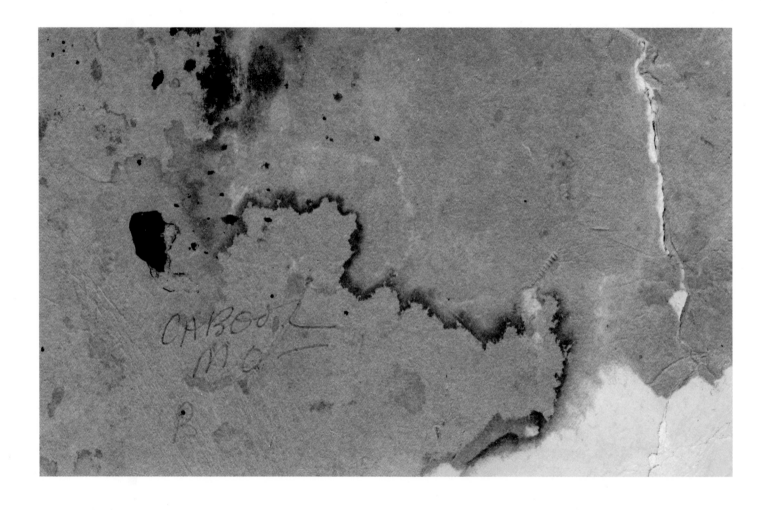

TAKE ME TO THE WATER

REVEREND E.D. CAMPBELL

Take me to the water,
Oh, take me to the water,
Oh, take me to the water and baptize me.

My brothers and sisters, we're down here today to celebrate this baptism. As you know, John the Baptist baptized Christ. Christ walked 72 miles and ordered John to baptize him. John said, "whose shoes I'm not worthy to unlatch, why have thou come to me for me to baptize thee?" The Lord said unto John, "suffer it to be so." John said alright and he went down in the water and baptized Christ. And God the Father, He left the void in the shape of a dove, come down on John, and it bored upon his shoulder, saying, "This is my beloved son in whom I'm well pleased." Bring the candidates on, brotheren, I'm gonna baptize 'em. In obedience, my dear brother, I baptize you upon your confession in the name of the Father, in the name of the Son, and the Holy Ghost. Amen.

None but the righteous,
Oh, none but the righteous
Oh, none but the righteous, shall see God.

Bring the candidates on, brotheren. My dear Sister, upon your confession I baptize you, name of the Father, name of the Son, and the Holy Ghost. Amen.

I want to ask the question. Is anybody here ever was baptized, when he let you down in the water, spirit of God got all in your hands, got all in your feet, got all in your soul, got your soul all [watered] with fire? My God is alright. He's a ball of fire, hmm, He's a ball of fire, hmm, He's a ball of fire burning in my soul. Ain't He alright, children? Sure enough, in conclusion meet me over yonder where parting happen no more. Then we can see our blessed Savior. Amen.

Black Billy Sun
Baptising at Fall

The negro on left had just been baptized and is on his way to change clothes - his god father follows.

AUG 24 1945

SISTER LUCY LEE

BILL BOYD AND HIS COWBOY RAMBLERS

When they baptized Sister Lucy Lee
Everybody in the country came out to see
And when old Parson Brown let Sister Lucy down
She hollered "Oh my goodness Parson don't let me drown!"
She nearly strangled
Then she rolled her eyes
"Please holy Parson that's where your duty lies."
They gave three cheers
And then they volunteered
When they baptized Sister Lucy Lee.

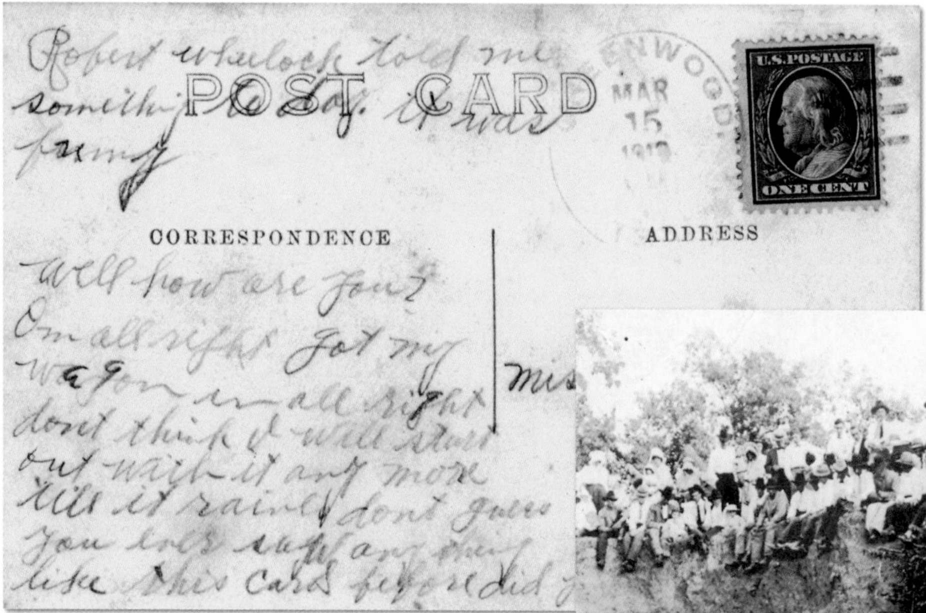

Robert wheelock told me something to day. it was funny

POST CARD

ENWOOD MAR 15 1912

U.S. POSTAGE ONE CENT

CORRESPONDENCE

ADDRESS

Well how are you? Im all right got my wagon in all right dont think I will start out with it any more till it rains dont guess you ever saw any thing like this card before did y

Mis

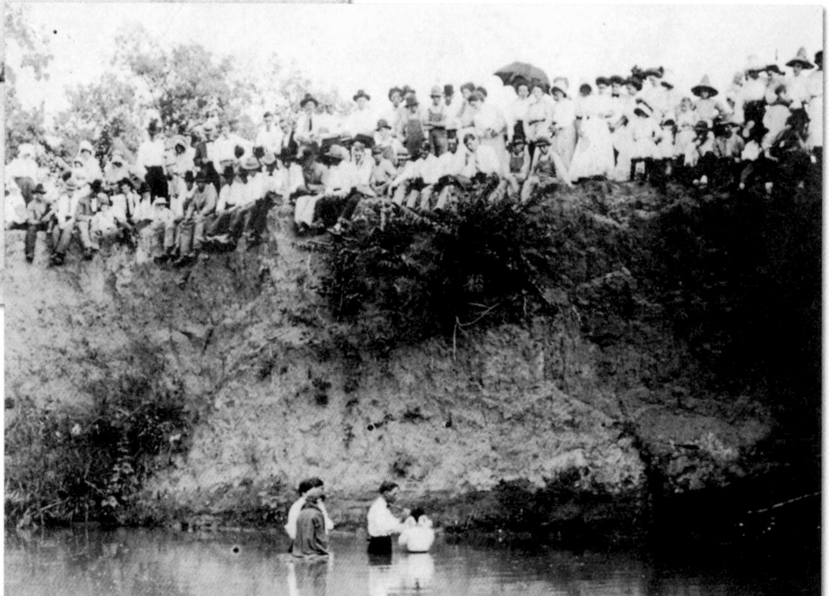

Baptism at Rockville W.Va.

Rockville
Preston Co
W.Va

BATHE IN THAT BEAUTIFUL POOL

Our fathers crossed over the river
They're now in the kingdom of God
They're now in the kingdom where the angels all dwell
Go wash in that beautiful pool

Go wash in that beautiful pool
Go wash in that beautiful pool
The rivers of life is flowing for all
Go wash in that beautiful pool

Our mothers crossed over the river
They're now in the kingdom of God
They're now in the kingdom where the angels all dwell
Go wash in that beautiful pool

Our sisters crossed over the river
They're now in the kingdom of God
They're now in the kingdom where the angels all dwell
Go wash in that beautiful pool

Dear Louise. We just got these pictures
recently. Mr Black has had such a
demand for them. From left to right
The Shart boy, Ed. Mamma, Mr Santen
Mrs Santen, Merl Santen & I have
forgotten the tiny girls name. The
children are always on hand at
prayer meeting with their verses
spoken so bravely. The minister.
is Mr Davis of First Baptist
Church of Eugene. Later he came
back & dedicated the Church. and
still later came for his vacation. mamma

Baptising in the Schoharie
river near Sloansville
1917

TWENTY-EIGHT SINNERS
GET RELIGION.-

PANTHERSVILLE, GA.---The Rev. GORDON
DON KELLEY, PASTOR OF THE CARMEL
CHRISTIAN CHURCH OF PANTHERSVILLE, GA.,
HOLDS A PUBLIC BAPTISM IN THE LOG CABIN
SWIMMING HOLE, OF CONVERTS AT A RECENT
REVIVAL.

POST CARD

CORRESPONDENCE HERE | NAME AND ADDRESS

Baptism in Cuyahoga
River 7-6-26

Baptizing Group
Vermont Mark ann Dexton in water
Sept 18 1910

Negro Baptism Tallulah, La.

Big Alum Pond   about 1894
Baptism Advent church
     Sturbridge MASS

POST CARD

△△▢○△
△ PLACE △
▯ STAMP ▯
○ HERE ○
△△▢○△

ENCE HERE | NAME AND ADDRESS HERE

John Benton Evans first ~~baptizing~~ ba...
Brother to Audrey's Grandad J. B. ...

this one is Lottie Gordon
going out. And Theron Brand
with rope
Baptising in the Schoharie river
near Sloansville
     1917

03 day of August 19...

BIBLICAL REFERENCE

MATTHEW 28:18–20
And Jesus came and spake unto them, saying, "All power is given unto me in heaven and in earth. Go ye therefore, and teach all nations, baptizing them in the name of the Father, and of the Son, and of the Holy Ghost: Teaching them to observe all things whatsoever I have commanded you: and, lo, I am with you always, even unto the end of the world. Amen."

ACTS 2:36–38
Therefore let all the house of Israel know assuredly, that God hath made that same Jesus, whom ye have crucified, both Lord and Christ. Now when they heard this, they were pricked in their heart, and said unto Peter and to the rest of the apostles, "Men and brethren, what shall we do?" Then Peter said unto them, "Repent, and be baptized every one of you in the name of Jesus Christ for the remission of sins, and ye shall receive the gift of the Holy Ghost."

MARK 1:8
I indeed have baptized you with water: but He shall baptize you with the Holy Ghost.

II KINGS 5:10–14
And Elisha sent a messenger unto him, saying, "Go and wash in Jordan seven times, and thy flesh shall come again to thee, and thou shalt be clean." But Naaman was wroth, and went away, and said, "Behold, I thought, He will surely come out to me, and stand, and call on the name of the Lord his God, and strike his hand over the place, and recover the leper. Are not Abana and Pharpar, rivers of Damascus, better than all the waters of Israel? May I not wash in them, and be clean?" So he turned and went away in a rage. And his servants came near, and spake unto him, and said, "My father, if the prophet had bid thee do some great thing, wouldest thou not have done it? How much rather then, when he saith to thee, 'Wash, and be clean?'" Then went he down, and dipped himself seven times in Jordan, according to the saying of the man of God: and his flesh came again like unto the flesh of a little child, and he was clean.

ISAIAH 1:16
Wash you, make you clean; put away the evil of your doings from before mine eyes; cease to do evil.

SONGS AND SERMONS

1. **Rev. J. M. Gates**
   Baptize Me
   Sermon with singing; with his congregation
   ca. September 1926; New York City

   I believe that a man and woman who has
   been borned again should be baptized. It is
   as much natural as it is for a little duck to
   desire water.

   Take me to the water
   Take me to the water
   Take me to the water
   Baptize me.

Rev. James M. Gates (July 14, 1884–August 18, 1945) of Atlanta, Georgia was the most prolifically recorded preacher by commercial record companies before World War II—making more than 200 records. In 1975, Roger S. Brown interviewed legendary A&R man/talent scout Polk Brockman about his involvement with Gates. Brockman stated: "Rev. J. M. Gates was without a doubt the most popular preacher of the time… So beloved was Rev. Gates that his funeral lasted three or four hours and drew a tremendous crowd." (*Living Blues*, September/October 1975)

2. **Washington Phillips**
   Denomination Blues part 1
   Vocal with novelty instrument.
   December 5, 1927; Dallas, Texas

The entire recorded output of George Washington Phillips (January 11, 1880–September 20, 1954) consists of 18 songs made between 1927 and 1929. Michael Corcoran shed some much-appreciated light on the mysterious musician and his otherworldly instrument in his December 29, 2002 article for the *Austin Statesman* entitled *Exhuming the Legend of Washington Phillips*. In the piece, ex-Simsboro, Texas resident Doris Foreman Nealy recalled the following about Phillips: "He was what they called a 'jack-leg preacher.' He didn't have a church, so he'd kinda roam the town looking for some place to preach. In Simsboro, we had a big picnic every June 19 and Mr. Wash would always start it off with a song. But none of us kids knew he ever made any records." Virgil Keeton, a former gospel quartet singer, recalled that Phillips "used to live in Simsboro with his mother. He used to play this harp-like instrument that he made himself. Sang like a bird, man." Virgil and his wife Jewell last remembered seeing Phillips in 1946 doing the devotion at St. James Methodist Church in Teague where he stated a phrase he often repeated: "I am born to preach the gospel, and I sure do love my job."

3. **Rev. Moses Mason**
   John the Baptist (Take 2)
   Vocal and guitar.
   ca. January 1928; Chicago, Illinois

   Jesus came from Nazarene unto Galilee
   To be baptized of John in Jordan
   And John said unto Him, Come and talk
   *   to me*

I need to be baptized of Thee
And Jesus said unto John, Suffer it to be so for
Thus it becomes us to fill all righteousness.

And John done saw that number
Way in the middle of the air.
Cryin' how long, how long, how long,
My Lord, oh how long.

After Jesus was baptized of John
Straightway out of the waters
Looked and saw heavens open
And the spirit of God came down
And lit a bow on Him, and Jesus was
Carried up into the mountain…

An advertisement in the March 17, 1928 *Chicago Defender* states that "Uncle Mose Mason, the singing elder from the Delta Land—now an exclusive Paramount artist—will inspire you and uplift you…" Little information is known about Mason, whose entire recording career consists of the eight songs he cut in Chicago in January 1928. Mason's version of "John the Baptist" which is included here also appears on the legendary *Anthology of American Folk Music* compiled by Harry Smith for Folkways Records in 1952.

4. Dock Walsh
Bathe in that Beautiful Pool
Vocal with banjo.
September 25, 1929; Memphis, Tennessee

"Go Wash in that Beautiful Pool" appeared for the first time in *Revival No. 2* (1896), a songbook by Charlie Davis Tillman (1861–1943). Wayne W. Daniel writes in *The New Georgia Encyclopedia* that Tillman was born in Tallassee, Alabama and exhibited a talent for music at a young age. He toured the revival circuit with his evangelist parents and participated in the musical portion of their services. As a young adult, Tillman struck out on his own and for 14 years pursued jobs as diverse as a house painter, an organ salesman, a medicine show performer and a minstrel show entrepreneur. He finally settled in Atlanta and returned to his religious work, primarily in the songwriting and music publishing fields.

5. Carter Family
On My Way to Canaan's Land
A. P. Carter, vocal; Sara Carter, autoharp, vocal; Maybelle Carter, guitar, vocal.
November 25, 1930; Memphis, Tennessee

Oh, be baptized in Jesus' name
Oh, be baptized in Jesus' name
Oh, be baptized in Jesus' name
I'm on my way, praise God, I'm on my way

Daphne Kilgore Stapleton, a close friend of Maybelle Addington (later Carter), recalls their baptism in *Will You Miss Me When I'm Gone?* (2004) by Mark Zwonitzer and Charles Hirshberg: "Baptism was on Copper Creek, down where Hugh M. Addington lived. There'd be all the people up on the hill watching, and buggies and horses. Wasn't hardly any cars back then. Maybelle and I were baptized at the same time, in 1924. There was a whole bunch of us baptized. There must have been about twelve or fifteen people. I was about thirteen, so Maybelle must have been about fifteen. Tom Carter baptized us."

6. Rev. R.M. Massey
Old Time Baptism part I
Sermon and singing; with congregation.
ca. January 1928; Chicago, Illinois

7. Rev. R.M. Massey
Old Time Baptism part II
Sermon and singing; with congregation.
ca. January 1928; Chicago, Illinois

David said, "If I had a thousand tongues,
I would praise God with all of them…"
You're willing to be baptized, you're willing
to be governed by the rules and regulations
of this church, stay on the firing line until
Jesus shall come…

You willing to be baptized? We're baptized over here, come to the bottom of the pool over here. You willing to be baptized?

This appears to be the only pre-WWII record to feature two sides that relate directly to the ceremony of baptism. Paul Oliver states in his book *Songsters and Saints* (1984) that Rev R. M. Massey was from Itta Bena, Mississippi. Because Moses Mason was in the Chicago studio at the same time as Massey, some researchers have speculated that Mason might have been from Mississippi, as well.

8. Southern Wonders Quartet
Go Wash in the Beautiful Stream
Probably Eugene Cunningham, lead; Guy Reynolds, tenor; James Huff, baritone; Randolph Butler, bass vocal, unaccompanied.
ca. July 24-26, 1940; New York City

Although several groups recorded under the Southern Wonders name, gospel music historians Ray Funk and Doug Seroff believe this recording is likely by a group from the Cleveland, Ohio area. A photo credit that appeared in the *Cleveland Call and Post* in May of 1942 describes the Southern Wonders as "wax artists with any number of records on display in the city."

James Huff is the only member of the Southern Wonders Quartet for which biographical information is known. Born to a minister's family in Comer, Georgia in 1906, Huff moved to Cleveland in 1923. He left the Southern Wonders Quartet, and in 1945 showed up with another Cleveland-area group —the Live Wire Singers.

In a telephone interview, Seroff pointed out that he hears a strong influence of the Birmingham quartet style in the Southern Wonders recordings, which he says can be attributed to the fact that Cleveland was a place to which many African Americans from the Jefferson County, Alabama area migrated.

9. Carolina Tar Heels
I'll Be Washed
Dock Walsh, banjo, vocal; Clarence "Tom" Ashley, guitar, vocal; Garley Foster, guitar.
November 14, 1928; Atlanta, Georgia

I'll meet you in that city of the new Jerusalem
I've been washed in the blood of the lamb

Doctor Coble Walsh (July 23, 1901–May 28, 1967) was born in Lewis Fork, Wilkes County, North Carolina. Nicknamed the "Banjo King of the Carolinas," he formed this version of the group's rotating lineup with Clarence "Tom" Ashley (1895–1968) on guitar/vocal and Garley Foster (1905–1968) on guitar. The stylistic difference between this performance and Walsh's solo slide banjo on track 4 is astounding. The Carolina Tar Heels often played minstrelsy arrangements like the one heard in "I'll Be Washed." The style likely came from Ashley's experience traveling with medicine shows.

10. Elder J. E. Burch
Wash You, Make You Clean (Take 2)
Sermon and singing with congregation, unknown tambourine, bass drum, snare drum, guitar.
October 23, 1927; Atlanta, Georgia

The subject in which we will use at this hour —it might seem a little common, but it's true. The subject is wash. You wash ladies understand that it's essential that you want your garments clean. And in the same like mind, our God almighty wants His garments clean. And He tells you to wash… Wash away your guilty conscience. Wash away every evil thought. And you don't wash, glory to God, with the natural water, but you wash with the word of God.

On October 23, 1927, Elder J. E. Burch recorded ten songs and sermons at his first and only recording session. Of the ten sides, only nine were issued, but a test pressing survives of the rejected recording. Upon listening to the first take of "Wash You, Make You Clean" it is easy to understand the engineer's decision: so enlivened in the spirit was Burch and his congregation that they continued their service as the recording space ran out. In both takes of the sermon, he presents followers with an option to "natural water" for cleansing themselves. Burch cites Ephesians 5:26: "That he might sanctify and cleanse it with the washing of water by the word." The second take when released went on to sell 3,629 copies.

11. Frank Jenkins of Da Costa Woltz's Southern Broadcasters
Babtist [sic] *Shout*
Banjo.
early May 1927; Richmond, Indiana

Frank Jenkins (1888–ca. 1945) was a banjo player and fiddler from Dobson, North Carolina. His three-finger picking exhibits the stops and starts characteristic of much old-time finger-picked banjo, without the never-ending rolls that later became a staple of bluegrass. The tuning, open D (f#DF#AD, here tuned up to g#EG#BE), is often associated with tunes of the "Reuben's Train" family, but "Shout" instead sounds like a genteel parlor piece. The tune's "feel" and the contours of its banjo rolls, especially in the second section (played as bar chords at the fifth and seventh frets) bear a resemblance to Kentuckian Pete Steele's classic "Coal Creek March," which is played with two fingers in the same tuning. *Special thanks to Christopher Berry for his contribution to this text.*

12. Tennessee Mountaineers
At the River
Mixed choir of 20 voices, unaccompanied.
August 5, 1927; Bristol, Tennessee

Shall we gather at the river,
Where bright angel feet have trod,
With its crystal tide forever
Yes, we'll gather at the river,
The beautiful, the beautiful river;
Gather with the saints at the river
That flows by the throne of God.

The Tennessee Mountaineers were a group of 20 singers, which included A. P. Carter's brother-in-law Roy Hobbs. Their entire recorded output of just two songs was etched in wax at the famous 1927 Bristol sessions. Often referred to as "The Big Bang of Country Music" because it marked the first recordings ever made by such talents as Jimmie Rodgers and the Carter Family, it would produce a more moderate seller with the Mountaineers pairing of "Standing on the Promises" and "At the River," which sold just 4,958 copies. "Standing on the Promises" appears on the *Goodbye, Babylon* set.

Robert Lowry (March 12, 1826–November 25, 1899) wrote "Shall We Gather at the River?" in 1864. First published in *Happy Voices* (1865), the song's words do not directly relate to a baptism ceremony, but the overall message does tie into the theme. Lowry's description of how he came to write the song displays a sea change of thought that likely inspired many songwriters after him:

One afternoon in July 1864, when I was pastor at Hanson Place Baptist Church, Brooklyn, the weather was oppressively hot, and I was lying on a lounge in a state of physical exhaustion… My imagination began to take itself wings. Visions of the future passed before me with startling vividness. The imagery of the apocalypse took the form of a tableau. Brightest of all were the throne, the heavenly river, and the gathering of the saints… I began to wonder why the hymn writers had said so much about the 'river of death' and so little about the 'pure water of life, clear as crystal, proceeding out of the throne of God and the lamb.' As I mused, the words began to construct themselves. They came first as a question of Christian inquiry, 'Shall we gather?' Then they broke in chorus, 'Yes, we'll gather.' On this question and answer the hymn developed itself. The music came with the hymn.

13. Empire Jubilee Quartet
Wade in de Water
probably Fred D. Young, First tenor; Andrew
D. Cole, Second tenor; Osmond L. Spaulding,
baritone; L.W. Bennett, bass vocal and
manager; unaccompanied.
July 29, 1929; Camden, New Jersey

Wade in de water
Wade in de water, go down
Wade in de water, children
Wade in de water and be baptized

Oh, look over yonder, what I see?
Wade in de water and be baptized
Oh, the Holy Ghost is coming on me
Wade in de water and be baptized

Little is known about the Empire Jubilee Quartet aside from a group by the same name appearing on radio program lists for WGBS 800 in the *New York Amsterdam News* in early 1928. The song, on the other hand, has been studied and interpreted for many years. In his book *Wade in the Water: The Wisdom of the Spirituals* (2005), Arthur Jones states "Wade in de Water" is a song composed for one purpose but it was used secretly for other, masked purposes. "This song was created to accompany the rite of baptism, but Harriet Tubman used it to communicate to fugitives escaping to the North that they be sure to 'wade in the water' in order to throw bloodhounds off their scent."

14. Rev. Nathan Smith's Burning Bush Sunday School Pupils
Baptism at Burning Bush
Sermon and singing.
September 5, 1935; Chicago, Illinois

Behold, I saw one coming
He was coming to be baptized

Amen. Sister House, this morning I'm
reminded of the time that Jesus walked
down to Jordan where John was baptizing.
Sister Mitchell, according to your profession,
I'll baptize you right now in the name of
the Father, the name of the Son, the name
of the Holy Ghost. Amen.

Wade, oh, wade in the water
I'm talking 'bout my Jesus, my heavenly
*   father*
Won't you wade, oh, wade in the water
Why won't you wade in the water to be
*   baptized?*

Rev. Nathan Smith made eight recordings in the span of a week during the only two sessions of his career. Only six recordings were issued, and in one he states he being from Marked Tree, Arkansas. Although there is no church in operation today in Marked Tree by that name, the Burning Bush Baptist Church in Memphis is just 37 miles away. It is unknown whether Smith's congregation used on this recording which features a simulated baptism is connected to that church.

15. Bill Boyd and His Cowboy Ramblers
Sister Lucy Lee
Curly Perrin, vocal; Jim Boyd, string bass; Bill
Boyd, guitar; Wilson "Lefty" Perkins, electric
steel guitar; John "Knocky" Parker, piano;
Muryel "Zeke" Campbell, electric guitar;
Marvin Montgomery, tenor banjo; unknown
drummer; Carroll Hubbard, fiddle; Kenneth
Pitts, fiddle; unknown third fiddle, unknown
drummer.
September 12, 1937; Dallas, Texas

William Lemuel Boyd (September 29, 1910–December 7, 1977) was born on the family's cattle ranch in Ladonia, Texas. Boyd and his three brothers began making music at early ages often honing their skills playing cowboy music when the day's chores on the ranch were complete. Word spread, and before long neighbors from near and far would drop in to hear the Boyd brothers play their Western-styled music. Around 1930, Boyd formed Bill Boyd and his Cowboy Ramblers. The group would go on to make more than 200 recordings and eventually settle into a successful career on radio.

16. Belmont Silvertone Jubilee Singers
Wade in the Water and Be Baptized
Vocal quartet, unaccompanied.
November 9, 1939; New York City

Little is known about the Belmont Silvertone Jubilee Singers other than, according to Ray Funk, they were possibly from Belmont, North Carolina which did have a quartet in the 1940s known as the Silvertones.

In his book *Slave Culture: Nationalist Theory and the Foundations of Black America* (1987), Sterling Stuckey writes about Simon Brown, who was born into slavery in Virginia in 1843. Brown recalled how slaves would "come from all 'roun'—in buggies an' carts an' on mule-back"—to attend revival meetings. "But mos' of them walk' on foot. The candidates for baptism would gather 'roun' an' march down the Big Road all dress' in white to the edge of the pond." Before the ceremony the congregation would sing a "'baptism' song," "one of the Deacons would hole in his han' a long staff built like a cross…would wade out into the water, usin' his staff as a soundin' stick in fron' of him. When the staff reach' the proper depth, he would drive it down hard into the bottom."

With the cross visible above the water, the preacher was "fetched" by the deacon and stood near it as the congregation sang:

Wade in the water, chillen
Oh, wade in the water, chillen,
Wade in the water, chillen,
Wade in the water to be baptize

Stuckey explains an African interpretation of the ceremony: "The staff made like a cross was, for the Bakongo, 'a tree across the water's path, a bridge that mystically put the dead and the living in perpetual communication.' In America, therefore, its retention was an illustration described by Simon Brown, of how a particular feature of the African religious vision, whatever the fate of its other features, might radiate the fullness of that vision without outsiders having the slightest awareness of its significance. So it was that the deacon in the ceremony was not simply a 'deacon' but 'the good leader' or priest who was capable of introducing the living to their ancestors through the ritual of water immersion."

17. Ernest Thompson
I'm Going Down to Jordan
Vocal with guitar and harmonica.
September 9, 1924; New York City

Ernest Errott Thompson (February 20, 1892–December 7, 1961) was born in Clemmons, North Carolina. In the book *String Bands in the North Carolina Piedmont* (2004), researcher Bob Carlin reprints an article from the April 28, 1924 edition of Winston-Salem's *Twin City Sentinel*, which describes how "a farmer living on a small track of land near Tobaccoville" came to be "an employee of the Columbia Phonograph Company, having made 44 records at the salary of $100 a week and expenses."

William S. Parks, regional representative of the Columbia Phonograph Company… came to Winston-Salem last Tuesday in his quest. He stopped by the Rominger Furniture Company and Mr. Rominger told him of one Ernest E. Thompson who was a born musician. Mr. Parks hopped into an automobile and drove out to Thompson's farm. There he discovered a blind man, sitting in the doorway of a humble home. The blind man was Thompson.

Sitting there in the warm April sunshine, Thompson played and sang a number of old southern melodies and folk songs. The more he played and more he sung, the more convinced was Mr. Parks that he had found the man he was looking for. It did not take much argument to persuade Thompson that he ought to go to New York immediately. He played before the officers of the Columbia Company there and they pronounced him great…"

18. Rev. J. C. Burnett
Go Wash in Jordan Seven Times
Sermon and Singing with Sisters Ethel Grainger And Odette Jackson
October 6, 1926; New York City

The June 18, 1927 edition of the *Pittsburgh Courier* features an article that reflects the success and humility of Rev. J. C. Burnett, a minister who research shows was probably from Kansas City, Missouri.

> *Rev. J. C. Burnett, Columbia Record artist, and in imitable exhorter of national repute, is now in the city as a guest of the Columbia Phonograph Company. Having been observed by a representative of Columbia and selected because of his unusual ability as a preacher, his first record was welcomed with the sale of about 400,000 records. His other numbers since then have also been met with popular approval by reason of the large number which have been purchased by the public. Rev. Burnett, as a recording artist, is considered to be in a class by himself… Those wishing to get in touch with the Reverend may do so by writing or calling at No. 9 Logan Street, where he is a guest of Mr. Jones.*

19. Birmingham Jubilee Singers
Wade in the Water
Charles Bridges, leader; Leo "Lot" Key, tenor; Dave Ausbrooks, baritone; James Ricks, bass vocal; unaccompanied.
March 20, 1930; Atlanta, Georgia

The Birmingham Jubilee Singers were organized in 1925 or '26 by Charles Bridges, who was Birmingham, Alabama's most important quartet trainer. They were the first Alabama quartet to tour outside of the state, and in 1926 they became the first group from Jefferson County to be recorded. Their training and recordings would influence many quartet groups in the area.

In 1929, the group's bass singer Ed Sherrill died in New York while on tour. James "Jimmy" Ricks of Philadelphia was singing with the Taskiana Four, and after that group broke up, Ricks was recruited to take Sherrill's place in the Birmingham Jubilee Singers. He accepted the invitation and moved to Jefferson County to join the group.

Dave Ausbrooks died in 1930, and the group was dissolved shortly thereafter. Bridges joined the Blue Jay Singers and led the successful group until they disbanded in the 1960s. Ricks also joined the Blue Jay Singers, then moved on to such groups as Flying Clouds of Detroit and the Golden Eagle Gospel Singers.

Special thanks to Doug Seroff for his contribution to this text.

20. J. E. Mainer's Mountaineers
Goin' Down to the River of Jordan
J. E. Mainer, fiddle and vocal; Junior Misenheimer, banjo; Harold Christy, guitar; Beacham Blackweller, guitar; Wade Mainer, vocal; Zeke Morris, vocal.
June 15, 1936; Charlotte, North Carolina

Joseph Emmett Mainer (July 20, 1898–June 12, 1971) and his brother Wade (born April 21, 1907) were born near Weaverville, North Carolina. When Wade was awarded an NEA National Heritage Fellowship in 1987 he said the following about his childhood: "It was kind of rough back in the days that I grew up. We were raised poor people back in the mountains, lived in an old log cabin, read the Bible at night by the old oil lamp."

Work in textile mills took J. E. to Knoxville, but the brothers would cross paths again in the 1930s in Concord, North Carolina where they each found jobs in a cotton mill. Reunited, they formed a string band with J. E. on fiddle and Wade on banjo. Playing social gatherings and fiddlers' conventions led to their 1934 /discovery by J. W. Fincher, the head of Crazy Water Crystals, who sponsored a barn dance radio show on WBT in Charlotte. Mainer's

Mountaineers growth in popularity brought invitations to play radio stations throughout the Southeast and eventually led to a recording contract with Bluebird Records.

RCA, the company that owned Bluebird, had the Carter Family's 1928 record "River of Jordan" with "Keep on the Sunny Side" in their back catalog. It was the best selling record of the Carter Family's career with more than 140,000 copies sold. With those kind of numbers, it is not surprising that they would want J. E. and Wade to record the same version of the song. The lyrics, although not specifically related to a baptism ceremony, would be reworked over time. When the Louvin Brothers recorded "River of Jordan" after World War II, they sang the following verses:

> To the River of Jordan our Savior went one day
> And we read that John the Baptist met Him there
> When John baptized Jesus in Jordan's rushing waters
> The mighty power of God filled the air
>
> I'm on my way to the River of Jordan
> Gonna wade right in to the rushing waters
> I'm going down to the River of Jordan
> And let the cool waters cleanse my soul

21. **Elder J. E. Burch**
Baptism by Water, and Baptism by the Holy Ghost
Sermon and singing, unknown tambourine, bass drum, snare drum, guitar.
October 23, 1927; Atlanta, Georgia

Paul Oliver notes in his book *Songsters and Saints* (1984) that Burch's session "can be considered virtually as a single, extended recording of a service, broken at three minute intervals and then reshuffled when issued on record, out of matrix sequence." His sermon "Wash You, Make You Clean" can be heard as track 10, and "My Heart Keeps Singing" appears on the *Goodbye, Babylon* box set.

22. **Moses Mason**
Go Wash in the Beautiful Stream
(Take 1)
Vocal and guitar.
ca. January 1928; Chicago, Illinois

Census information shows more than 20 men named Mose or Moses Mason living in Louisiana and Mississippi around the time of this recording. One potential lead comes from Mason's recording of "Red Cross the Disciple of Christ Today," in which he makes a reference to Greenville, Mississippi, where there was a Red Cross refugee camp at the time.

23. **Sunset Four Jubilee Singers**
Wade in the Water
Andy Bryant, first tenor and leader; Leonard Burton, second tenor; Fred J. Vaughan, baritone; William "Hoss" Crawford, bass vocal.
ca. April 1925; Chicago, Illinois

Andrew E. Bryant, the leader of the Sunset Four Jubilee Singers was from Columbus, Ohio. In 1916, he toured with the Florida Troubadours, and a year later he went out with the Old Fashioned Four. In the early 1920's, Bryant sang with Buckner's Jubliee Singers before starting a new group in 1923 called the Four Sons of Ham, which was later renamed the Sunset Four.

When bass vocalist William Buckner left the group in late 1924 to take a group of singers to Australia and New Zealand, Bryant recruited Hoss Crawford, with whom he had sung in the Old Fashioned Four. Hoss told the *Chicago Defender* that "he had no trouble whatever joining in with the boys at quick notice." The group toured the Midwest in their own car in the early 1920s, which was uncommon for the time. Reports from their touring, such as the following, often appeared in the *Chicago Defender*:

> Sunset Four, one of the best of present-day quartets, is a great hit on Road Show No. 8

traveling over the west end of the big time. The line-up carries Andy Bryant, Leonard Burton, Fred Vaughn and Hoss Crawford. Here is what a San Bernardino newspaper said of them last week:

The Sunset Four, billed as eight hundred pounds of harmony, four colored boys who could sing, was the hit of the show. They took several encores and could have taken more. Their offering in harmony is one that typifies the American Negro. Most of the songs were more or less original, and several of a religious nature, but the harmony and their showmanship method of putting it over took the audience. Their imitation of the 'steam calliope' was an instantaneous hit. The eight hundred pounds of weight was more or less between the tenor and bass singers, but the harmony was equally divided.
— December 13, 1924 edition of Chicago Defender

24. Ernest Stoneman's Dixie Mountaineers
Down to Jordan and Be Saved
Uncle Eck Dunford, fiddle, vocal; Ernest V. Stoneman, harmonica, guitar, vocal; unknown second fiddle.
October 31, 1928; Bristol, Tennessee

Alex "Uncle Eck" Dunford (1878–1953) was a fiddler, guitarist, vocalist and storyteller. Tony Russell describes Dunford in his book *Country Music Originals: The Legends and the Lost* (2007) as someone "whose brogue seems to place him in another century, not so much old-time as Old Father Time." Ernest V. Stoneman (1893–1968) sings "There's a Light Lit up in Galilee" on the reverse side of this record, which appears on the *Goodbye, Babylon* box set.

25. Rev. E. D. Campbell
Take Me to the Water
Sermon; assisted by Sisters Watkins and Dunlap and Brother Griffin
February 26, 1927; Memphis, Tennessee

This track, which record label files show sold 12,036 copies, also appears on *Goodbye, Babylon*. Musicologist and researcher David Evans wrote the following annotation for the 2003 gospel box set:

Rev. E. D. Campbell is probably the Rev. Eugene D. Campbell, who is reported in the Memphis City Directory between 1929 and 1933, listed in 1932 as pastor of the Ash Grove Missionary Baptist Church. Whether he was living in Memphis in 1927, when he first recorded there, is unknown. He appears to have been Victor Records hoped-for rival to

Rev. J. M. Gates in early 1927, as the company promoted his initial records with some success, but most of his sermons are somewhat lacking in coherence, revealing him as probably little more than a typical "jack-leg" preacher. "Take Me to the Water" is one of his best efforts, being the recreation of a baptizing ceremony, complete with the tune that one usually hears at old-time baptisms. Campbell's mention of "a ball of fire burning in my soul" at the end of the record suggests the influence of sanctified doctrines. Such influences were especially prevalent in Memphis, which was the headquarters of the largest sanctified denomination, the Church of God in Christ.

Since the publication of Dr. Evans research in 2003 we have learned from record label session sheets that Campbell was in fact a Memphis resident when he recorded this sermon.

BIBLIOGRAPHY

Allen, James, Hilton Als, Jon Lewis and Leon F. Litwack. *Without Sanctuary: Lynching Photography in America*. Santa Fe: Twin Palms, 1999.

Carlin, Bob. *String Bands in the North Carolina Piedmont*. Jefferson, North Carolina: McFarland, 2004.

Corcoran, Michael. *Exhuming the Legend Of Washington Phillips*. Austin Statesman, Dec. 29, 2002.

Daniel, Wayne W. *Charlie D. Tillman (1861–1943)*. The New Georgia Encyclopedia. May 9, 2003. http://www.georgiaencyclopedia.org/nge/Article.jsp?id=h-888

Dixon, Robert M.W. and John Godrich. *Blues & Gospel Records, 1902–1942*. 3rd ed. Chigwell, Essex: Storyville Publications, 1982.

Evans, David, Dick Spottswood and others. *Goodbye, Babylon*. Atlanta: Dust-to-Digital, 2003.

Jones, Arthur and Donna Auguste. *Wade in the Water: The Wisdom of the Spirituals*. Denver: Leave a Little Room Foundation, 2005.

Lowry, Robert. *Happy Voices*. New York: American Tract Society, 1865.

Meade, Guthrie T., Dick Spottswood, and Douglas S. Meade. *Country Music Sources: A Biblio-Discography of Commercially Recorded Traditional Music*. Chapel Hill: University of North Carolina Press, 2002.

Oliver, Paul. *Songsters & Saints: Vocal Traditions on Race Records*. Cambridge: Cambridge University Press, England, 1984.

Russell, Tony. *Country Music Originals: The Legends and the Lost*. New York: Oxford University Press US, 2007.

Russell, Tony. *Country Music Records: A Discography, 1921–1942*. New York City: Oxford University Press US, 2004.

Scarborough, Dorothy and Ola Lee Gulledge. *On the Trail of Negro Folk-Songs*. Cambridge: Harvard University Press 1925.

Stuckey, Sterling. *Slave Culture: Nationalist Theory and the Foundations of Black America*. New York: Oxford University Press US, 1987.

Tribe, Ivan M. *The Stonemans: An Appalachian Family and the Music that Shaped Their Lives*. Chicago: University of Illinois Press, 1993.

Zwonitzer, Mark and Charles Hirshberg. *Will You Miss Me When I'm Gone?: The Carter Family & Their Legacy in American Music*. New York: Simon and Schuster, 2004.

CREDITS

Collection produced by: Steven Lance Ledbetter and Jim Linderman
Essays: Jim Linderman and Luc Sante
Notes on songs and sermons: Steven Lance Ledbetter
Biblical reference: Steven Lance Ledbetter

Art direction and design: John Hubbard and Rob Millis
Photographs scanned by: April G. Ledbetter

Original 78s: Joe Bussard, Steven Lance Ledbetter, Frank Mare and
  Roger Misiewicz
Audio restoration and mastering: Robert Vosgien, Capitol Mastering
Record transfers: David Anderson, Michael Graves and John Wilby
Song transcriptions: April G. Ledbetter, Steven Lance Ledbetter
  and Rob Millis

The audio portion of this collection is derived from extremely rare
records, which have been remastered to produce the best possible
sound. We believe the historical and musical importance outweigh the
imperfections and noise in the original recordings.

Special thanks: Susan Archie, Agnieszka Czeblakow, Dr. David Evans,
  Ray Funk, Jesse Austin Morris, Christopher Berry, Dr. Guido van
  Rijn, Tony Russell, Doug Seroff and Malcolm Vidrine

All photographs are in the collection of the International Center of
  Photography, Gift of Janna Rosenkranz and Jim Linderman, 2007.
Accession numbers 2007.107.1–2007.107-196

As far as can be determined, other than brief notes on the reverse of
some images (some of which are included in this book), no record or
documentation exists for these photographs. They were found in flea
markets, auctions, antique shows and such over the last 20 years.

This book was printed in China by C&C Offset Printing Co., Ltd.
Color separations by iocolor, Seattle
ISBN 978-0-9817342-1-7

This release ©℗2009 Dust-to-Digital. Components under license
  from various sources.

Dust-to-Digital
PO Box 54743
Atlanta, GA 30308-0743
info@dust-digital.com

International Center of Photography
1133 Avenue of the Americas at 43rd Street
New York, NY 10036
info@icp.org

DATE DUE
